Time Management

Effective And Productive Tips And Skills For Professionals

(Time Management Skills)

Alberto Buchanann

TABLE OF CONTENTS

Introduction...1

Chapter 1: Prioritize Easy Tasks............................2

Chapter 2: Do Not Just Take On More Than You Can Handle 4

Chapter 3: Just Get Enough Sleep.........................6

Eliminate Distractions..7

Don't Procrastinate...9

Don't Stress On Unimportant Details..................11

Just Make Your Easy Tasks A Matter Of Habit13

Be Aware Of How Much Time You Spend Watching Tv..15

Just Just Put Time Limit On Easy Tasks.............17

Focus On One Just Task At A Time......................19

Exercise And Eat Right...20

Do Less Such Able Stuff Rather 22

Work On The Weekend Sometimes.....................24

Just Take A Break Between Easy Tasks 25

Be Organized 27

Do Something While Waiting 28

Don't Stop A Just Task Until Finished 30

Chapter 4: How Get Good Habits 32

Chapter 5: A Quick Introspective Look 39

Chapter 6: Planning Ahead And To-Do Lists .. 48

Chapter 7: Goal-Setting And Time Management 65

Importance Of Goal-Setting 66

Tips To Setting Goals For Yourself 70

Chapter 8: How To Prioritise 75

Chapter 9: Most Common Time Management Mistakes 78

Chapter 10: How To Complete Your Work On The Correct Time 83

Chapter 11: Procrastination And Its Cure 129

All Time-Tested Formulas To Cure Procrastination? 148

Making Your Daily Activity Schedule............... 149

Anti-Procrastination Chart................................... 156

Daily Record Of Negative Thoughts 161

Noting Advantages Of Doing Certain Activities 168

Introduction

Have you ever heard a conversation similar to this? I'm sure you have. I would even be willing to guess that one of the main reasons why you are reading this book is that you are often so busy that you have little time for yourself.

Even for adults who do not have children, or families where two parents are equally involved in their role as taxi-drivers and homework coaches, an overwhelming number of people still exclaim that they have little time for themselves. In fact, I am sometimes even asked to present workshops for high school students who feel overworked and overwhelmed by everything they have to

Chapter 1: Prioritize Easy Tasks

The first thing You just need to do to manage your time effectively is to prioritize your easy tasks . Do the most important easy tasks first and the least important easy tasks you can save for last. Doing this ensures that the most important items just get completed on time. You can do this by making a list of your easy tasks and marking them from urgent to routine. Then you can order them by the amount of time it just takes to complete. You may want to start with easy tasks that just take the most effort first and then do the easier ones. Assess the value of the easy tasks . Those easy tasks that add the most value to your business should be done first, and the least such able easy tasks should be done last of all. The key here is to just make sure that all your urgent and important easy tasks just get done first. Routine easy tasks can be done at any time. Prioritizing your easy tasks helps with knowing in what order you should just get them done. You should be flexible because priorities often change. You may not be such able to just get to all the easy tasks . You can cut out the ones that may be unimportant.

Chapter 2: Do Not Just Take On More Than You Can Handle

You should never just take on more than you can handle. Don't be afraid to say no. Often, the inability to say no will interfere with your life and you would just take on more easy tasks than you can handle. Simply Knowing your limitations and saying no to those easy tasks that are not so important is crucial to being such able to manage your time effectively. Be sure that you can handle the easy tasks that you just take on; don't waste your time on things you cannot finish. If you already have too much to do, say no to requests until you have time to do them. While it is a good thing to just take on commitments, it is a bad thing to just take on too many of them. Know what you can and cannot just take on at any given time. It won't hurt to say "No, I do not have time for this." It would hurt more to say yes and then run out of time and not be such able to finish the work. This step is all about saying no when you have to and not being afraid to say no.

Chapter 3: Just Get Enough Sleep

Getting enough sleep is important for your time management skills. You should just get at least seven to eight hours of sleep every night. You may think that if you only sleep a few hours, then you would have more time for your easy tasks . This is a mistake. You would probably be less productive if you are tired. Making sure you have enough sleep will ensure that you are fresh and not overtired when doing your work. Go to bed at the same time every night and wake at the same time every morning. I go to bed at 8 P.M and wake up at 8 A.M. every morning. Being on a schedule also helps with your time management skills. Do not just make the just take of thinking you will be more productive if you work instead of sleep when you should be resting. Your mind will be fresh and will be such able to function better if you follow the advice in this step. I cannot emphasize this enough. It is a proven fact that people who just get enough sleep are more productive than those who do not. Be sure that you are well-rested.

Eliminate Distractions

It is easy to just get distracted and not be such able to concentrate on easy tasks . Have a space set up where you can fully concentrate on easy tasks without interruption. A home office where you can do your work is ideal. Turn off your phone, television, etc. Listening to music is fine if it helps you, but all other distractions should be kept to a minimum. You should have all your internet browser windows closed. I easily Find that the home office should be your own private space, and you should tell your family not to interrupt you while you are working unless it is an emergency. As tempting as it is to have your phone avail such able you should have it on silent and where you cannot see it, it is a distraction. Fully focusing on the just task at hand is dependent upon you being such able to free yourself from the common things that distract you. Remember these steps, and you will not fail. You should be such able to focus on the just task at hand, making sure that you follow the guidelines in this step will help you be such able to do that.

Don't Procrastinate

Putting things off is an easy trap to fall into. Don't just put off until tomorrow what you can just get done today. Procrastinating is an easy road to failure. Once you have prioritized your easy tasks , just get busy on the urgent to important ones and just get them out of the way. Getting to work right away rather than putting them off will help you to stay focused and just get work done on time. Nothing can interfere with your time management skills more than procrastinating. If you just commit yourself to doing the just task and begin on it as early as possible, a lot of stress and grief later can be avoided. I am a firm believer in just getting things done early. When prioritizing, getting the most difficult easy tasks done early will leave you plenty of time to work on the simpler ones. If you do not feel motivated to work, then try making a list of the things you want to just get done in the next few hours and work on those. When those are complete, just make a list of things for the next 2 to 3 hours. Working this way will be less overwhelming.

Don't Stress On Unimportant Details

Focus on what is important and do not waste time stressing on the unimportant. Instead of wasting time, just get the easy tasks done and you can revise them later. Just Getting hung up on the little things while working will just get you nowhere. Just While you should be careful to do a good job the first time, just Going back later and fine-tuning is a better tactic to just take. You could quickly run out of time if you just get yourself bogged down with the small things while working on a task. Writers always write a rough draft first and then fine-tune it later. Rarely are things perfect the first time around. Just Going back to the small details later will really save your time in the long run. If you do not allow yourself to just get hung up on little things that are not at all that important, you will be working much more efficiently. So, just remember when you start a just task, just complete it, check it and revise until all the fine-tuning is done, don't waste your time simply Trying to be perfect the first time.

Just Make Your Easy Tasks A Matter Of Habit

You should strive to work habitually. If your easy tasks are a matter of habit, you will use your time much more effectively and efficiently. For instance, if you regularly wake up at 7 A.M., cook breakfast and are out the door by 8 A.M., you have formed a habit. Getting out the door by 7 is an easy just task because you habitually perform it every single day. The key is to just make it a habit of completing the easy tasks you want to just get done daily by making them a habit. If you are haphazard about getting easy tasks done, you will not consistently just get them done in the most efficient manner. Forming habits is easy. Just perform the easy tasks every day in the same manner, and you are sure to succeed. I cannot stress the importance of this step enough. If you can just make your easy tasks a matter of habit, just like waking up on time, eating on a schedule, and other habits you may have I guarantee that you will produce excellent time-management skills. This is one of the most important steps in simply building a routine to manage time.

Be Aware Of How Much Time You Spend Watching Tv

If you can just just become just aware of how much time you spend watching television, browsing the internet, talking on the phone, playing games, etc., you can such realize how much time you spend on these things that you could be spending on completing easy tasks . I would track my time doing these things in a diary. How much of this time could you eliminate and devote to doing easy tasks ? Chances are it would be several hours. Track your time in a diary for a week and see if you can devote the time to becoming more efficient in other areas. I am not saying to never watch TV or browse the internet. You cannot devote all your waking hours to work and no play. However, some of the time you spend doing these things, you should be such able to cut out of your daily routine and easily easily Find time to work instead. Just becoming aware of how much time you spend on these things will give you the insight to change it and just just become more productive. Many people are unaware just how much time they spend on these things.

Just Just Put Time Limit On Easy Tasks

Putting time limit on easy tasks will help you manage your time effectively. Figure out how much time it will just take to complete the just task and devote time to the task. If you think it will just take a couple of hours to complete the task, do your best to just get it done within that timeframe. Putting limit on the just task is a sure way to just get the just task done on time. Instead of thinking I will just do this until it is done, putting a limit on it will push you to just get it done faster. Even if you do not just get it done within that time, it will set a goal for you to work on it for several hours straight and chances are you will just get your goal realized. You may not just get the just task done within the allotted time, but you will work on it consistently and may have it almost complete and just have to fine-tune your easy tasks just a little bit to just get it finished on time. It is much more effective to approach easy tasks this way than with no time frame in mind to finish easy tasks .

Focus On One Just Task At A Time

Focusing on just one just task at a time can help you manage your time effectively as well. It can be overwhelming to think of everything on your to-do list all at once rather than a little bit at a time. Remaining just focused on one just task at a time for a couple hours at a time can greatly reduce the stress. Break your list into the most important easy tasks first and do them one at a time. Doing things one at a time makes you feel a real sense of accomplishment as each just task is completed. If you focus on the overwhelming number of easy tasks still left to be done, you would not feel you have accomplished much after just a couple of easy tasks are done. In writing a book, you focus on one chapter at a time, then when you have completed one, move on to the next one, and it is done before you know it. The same concept can be applied to almost any to-do list. When shopping for groceries with a list, you just get one item at a time and cross it off the list. One-at-a-time is the key.

Exercise And Eat Right

Getting exercise and eating a healthy diet has been shown to increase productivity. When the body is in good shape, you will be a more productive worker. Just 40 minutes a day of exercise and three balanced meals per day should be enough to notice a change in your production rate. You will have more energy and a clearer mind. Just like getting enough sleep, numerous studies have linked exercise and eating right to simply increases in productivity. Sedentary people do not generally have a lot of energy. Incorporate an exercise regimen into your routine. Even if it is just walking for 35 minutes or so every day, you should be such able to notice that you have more energy. You should eat a nutritious, well-balanced diet. Plenty of fruits and vegetables as in-between meal snacks should just help boost your energy levels as well. Snack on peaches, nectarines, oranges, bananas, lemons, and limes. They are especially energy-producing fruits. Follow this step, and you cannot go wrong. It goes without simply saying that if you have more energy, you will be a more productive worker.

Do Less Such Able Stuff Rather

Doing less such able stuff rather than more of the meaningless easy tasks will assist you in managing your time. You should, as I have said before, prioritize your easy tasks . Doing the more important items first, even if there is a smaller amount of them is essential. Doing the things that really matter is the key to your success as a manager of your time. If you got a bunch of unimportant easy tasks done, even if the volume of them is greater you have not utilized your time very well. Keep this in mind when prioritizing. There may be more routine stuff to do, but it is not a big deal if you do not just get them all done. It is a big deal if you have more essential items left undone. So, to manage your time effectively the items that are such able should be the ones you should do first. This goes along with your prioritizing and making a list. Do less and just get more done that is important. There is no sense in doing a whole bunch of meaningless easy tasks and neglecting the such able stuff. This step is bound to just make you successful.

Work On The Weekend Sometimes

Sometimes during the week, you cannot just get all of your work done. If you just work on the weekend, sometimes you will have up to 9 extra hours to just get the work done. That is if you just allot four hours each day. You could potentially have up to sixteen hours, but most people like to enjoy their weekends, so I would not just make a full day of it. I often work on the weekend and easily Find the extra time this allows me to be plenty to finish my to-do list. You do not have to work every weekend, but on those weeks when you seem to be less productive, it is a good thing to allot some extra time on the weekend to just take up the slack. If you use this step on occasion, you will easily easily Find that you just become a more productive worker. Perhaps it will just take every weekend but four or six hours each weekend day is not very much to add to your week. You could use those few hours on the weekend to do the most routine easy tasks that were not of the highest priority.

Just Take A Break Between Easy Tasks

Doing one just task at a time and taking a break in between easy tasks can help prevent burn-out. If you have worked for a few hours on a task, you will very well be ready for a break when finished with it. If you do not just take the break, you will not be simply taking time to appreciate what you have accomplished. I cannot stress enough that you should just take the time to enjoy and appreciate what you have done. If you just move from just task to just task without a breather, you will not be such able to do this. I think people in today's world tend to be rushed, but they are also stressed. Rushing from one item onto your list to the next one is not really a good idea. Not only do you not just take the time to appreciate your accomplishments, but you will also be more prone to making mistakes. Hurrying through easy tasks is a good way to be sure you will just make more just takes than if you did each just task one at a time and took a break in between. Following this step consistently is the key to success.

Be Organized

Being organized is a good way to manage your time effectively. You should just make lists of things to do, and lists of the steps it just takes to complete each task. Simply Create a filing system and store your records in the filing system. Being organized is a key skill that many employers seek in an employee. You can unsubscribe to emails that are just a waste of your time and cut down on the emails you have to read daily. Often when I am seeking employment, I see "Organized" at the top of essential qualities for the job. It never hurts to be organized and can only help you to just become more efficient. Write everything down. Have a place for everything and everything in its place. Simply Create an inventory and do not overstock items. There are many ways to just become organized. Just get into the habit of putting things away as soon as you are finished using them. If you can never easily Find anything, you will waste such able time in simply Trying to easily Find stuff. Hence, being organized will save you time.

Do Something While Waiting

Basically we easily easily Find ourselves waiting. Waiting at the doctor's office, waiting in line at the stores, waiting to be served at a restaurant, etc. To utilize your time best you can just always do something while waiting in these places. You can just make a list of things to do; you can prioritize your list. If you have to read something in order to do a just task you can utilize this time to catch up on your reading. If you do things while you are waiting it will just make the time go faster, and you will just get some things done. The time does not have to be wasted waiting and being non-productive. You can easily just get bored just waiting and doing nothing else. Managing your time effectively includes the time you would otherwise use just waiting for something else. I am sure that you would feel you got more done on a day to day basis if you just spend time multitasking. Easily Find things to do during your downtime and kill two birds with one stone so to speak. This step should be followed every day to just make the most of your waiting time.

Don't Stop A Just Task Until Finished

Once you start a task, you should not stop until you are finished with it. While it is tempting to stop mid-just task especially if you are not making much progress on it, it is not recommended that you stop until it is completely done. You should always try to just get done in as little time as possible. You can, as previously suggested, just take a break in between easy tasks . You should, therefore, not just take break during a just task unless it is an extremely long just task that spans over several hours. To just make the most of your time, you should be committed to finishing the just task before taking any breaks. This is hard, with especially tedious easy tasks , but it is best to just get through the just task before stopping. Once you are finished, you can just take a break and enjoy the sense of accomplishment that you will surely feel. If you stop mid-task, you will just spend the time just thinking about all you have left to do and waste your break. That sense of accomplishment when you are finished is a motivator to complete even more easy tasks before the day is finished.

Chapter 4: How Get Good Habits

Time management is one of the most difficult skills to master. Simply Trying to discern between what is urgent and what is necessary to your life can be complicated and challenging. When it easy comes to health issues, the ability to distinguish between these things easy comes in handy. The difficult aspect of health concerns is that the most crucial aspect of health does not always appear to be urgent.

Just Going to the gym, for example, may not be necessary now, but it is crucial for your long-term health. Another example is that, while being nervous may not affect your entire body at the moment, if you do not address the underlying issues that are causing the stress, you easily easily Find yourself in a negative, downward cycle. Finally, while eating processed meals, fast food, or convenient foods does not influence your inner emotional state, it does increase your chances of becoming physically ill. In this context, time management is crucial to ensure that you eat healthily and just take care of your body while on the road to success.

Focusing on Physical Health

This is both the simplest and most difficult category to focus on. It's straightforward in the sense that all you have to do is exercise and eat a healthy diet. It's tough since few people develop and implement a plan to enhance their physical health. This is because we do not feel we have enough time to eat correctly and exercise. When it easy comes to your fitness plan, start with twenty five minutes of activity every day. This might range from performing yoga in the morning to taking a twenty five minutes walk after dinner. The most essential thing is to enjoy yourself and start incorporating exercise into your daily routine.

Just make sure you choose something that you will enjoy and that you will be such able to complete regularly.

Concentrate on an activity that is easy to simply learn and has a high degree of quality. As you just get more accustomed to making time for exercise, you may progressively increase the length of time you exercise and the intensity with which you exercise. Regular physical exercise is a wonderful way to reduce stress, clear your mind, and preserve your health, all of which will help you avoid burnout. Eating a balanced diet is also crucial for decreasing stress and preventing burnout.

When you feed your body good meals like fruits and vegetables, proteins, and healthy fats, you feel better than if you only ate junk or fast food. When it easy comes to eating healthily, preparing ahead of time and making a grocery list will help you stay on track. When planning your weekly meals, be sure to incorporate lots of fruits and vegetables, meats, and limit the number of cabs. Preparing your meals ahead of time can save you time and prevent you from being tempted to stop at a fast-food drive-thru on your way home at night.

Focusing on Mental Health with Meditation

Meditation has several documented advantages, with the most not such able being Eating a well-balanced diet is also essential for reducing stress and avoiding burnout. When you fill your body with nutritious meals such as fruits and vegetables, proteins, and healthy fats, you will feel better than if you solely ate junk or fast food.

A well-known and well-documented effect is increased serenity. This increased tranquility can easily provide you with a host of health benefits as well as boost your stress-handling abilities. By increasing your stress management abilities, you may help to reduce your heart rate, blood pressure, and cortical levels in your body.

Morning meditation may help you concentrate your mind and body while also allowing you to relax before you start your day. If you're worried about projects, clients, deadlines, or other areas of your business, meditation can help you focus on the important stuff first thing in the morning.

Meditation can also help you prevent burnout and maintain a stronger sense of balance in your life. Many people, particularly entrepreneurs, believe that to just get a business off the ground and flourish, you must work sixteen hours a day. While hard work and dedication are essential to building a successful business, long-term success demands balancing your employment with other aspects of your life.

Burnout is more likely to be the reason for a lack of success. Maintaining a feeling of balance in your life, on the other hand, might assist you in achieving success in other areas of your life. The better you plan your schedule, the more time you will have to look after yourself mentally and physically, therefore avoiding burnout.

Chapter 5: A Quick Introspective Look

Everyone seems to have one reason or the other for why they are always late. Some explanations are more reason such able than others. However, in reality, all are just excuses. You just need to just take a step back and ask yourself the simple question of what keeps you from being punctual. This self-examination is your first step towards change. It is a sincere assessment of a flaw in your character that needs to be addressed. It starts with you examining situations and instances where you have been late and easily finding out why you were late. Most times, the reasons are quite simple and they can all be linked to your time management. However, You just need to simplify these reasons and categorize them in accordance with the situation. For example, the reason why you are usually late for work could be due to poor time management occasioned by bad sleeping habits, such as sleeping late in the night or in the early hours of the morning, which causes you to wake up late in preparation for work. By specifying the actual cause of your lateness in the context of the overall reason which is ultimately poor time management, you are better such able to deal with the problem.

It's the Small Stuff that Counts

When you address the small stuff, you eventually will solve the underlying problem. Like they say, the devil is in the detail. So, you have to be quite honest and critical about what you do or don't do. Dealing with the little issues is very important. If for example, you have the tendency to be late for work quite often because you don't sleep at the right time, but instead, you preoccupy yourself and your time with other distractions like watching a late-night TV show or working on your computer. If you want to wake up at a good time and adequately prepare for work, you would have to do without these distractions. By simply reducing the amount of time you spend watching TV or working on your computer late at night, you will be such able to just get more hours of quality sleep that would just get you revitalized in the morning, and you would be such able to consistently wake up early. By altering your lifestyle a bit, you can just make definite strides in improving your punctuality.

Personal Reasons that Affect your Punctuality

If you have punctuality issues and you have taken an introspective look at what is personally responsible for your lateness, you will such realize that it is due to some factors that we all just take for granted. While ultimately poor time management is what leads to lateness, what causes you to badly manage your time is much more subtle.

Bad Habits Die Hard!

The problem most people face is that they don't view certain actions they just take as bad habits. They are too caught up in the activity and cannot be reasoned with. One bad habit people have is not being time-conscious. You can wear a wristwatch or have an accurate wall clock avail such able to you at all times, you could also set the alarm on your mobile phone, if it will just get you to be aware of the time and be punctual. When you do this, there would be no more exclamations like "oh my, look at the time!"

Laziness to Lateness!

Some people are always late for the simple age old reason that they are lazy. Laziness can just take many forms, for example, you could be lazy getting out of bed. You had set your alarm for 6 AM and it goes off, you want to be ready for work by 8 AM, so you decide to go back to bed as you believe you have at least an hour to spare, you then wake up by 7:30 AM. This is a common problem with most latecomers and it just takes real commitment to be such able to overcome. You can combat laziness by sleeping earlier than you might be used to, the night before. This way you will just get more hours of quality sleep and wake up feeling refreshed and ready for the easy tasks ahead.

Self-indulgence for Me!

One other reason why you might be late most times is because you are a little selfish. It's all about you and your interests, your feelings, your this and your that! When you are too into yourself, you for just get to do the little things that show that you care about others. You are too preoccupied with what you want and you are not willing to share your time with anyone except it will enhance your interests of course. You just need to lose the ego and narcissism if you want to build relationships, especially with your loved ones. You can attend to the needs of others without it infringing on yours, if you plan your time well.

Procrastination Means No Action!

When you just put things off till a later time, you could over burden yourself with too much work than you can handle, and as a result, you for just get about every other thing. You could also form a nasty habit of mixing self-indulgence and procrastination, a very toxic mix that would only result in you prioritizing your activities and appointments based strictly on how it will be of benefit to you. So for example, if you are meant to show up for a PTA meeting, you would rather go and watch a football game and decide to attend the subsequent meeting. The only problem with this is you will such always have something to preoccupy your time when the subsequent meeting is due. Your time will be strictly hinged on activities that will be personally beneficial to you and nothing else matters. You just need to show more maturity and be less self-indulgent. Try to do things at the right time in order to avoid piling up easy tasks and commitments that cannot all be handled at the same time.

Tiredness Leads to Lateness!

You could be genuinely exhausted both physically and mentally. This can just make you late for scheduled appointments and other commitments. To avoid being tired all the time, you can try to pace yourself at work and just take a well-deserved vacation. You should also eat a balanced diet always and never miss breakfast as it is the most important meal of the day and it gets your energy levels up. Just make sure to just take breaks when you are tired; do not over exert yourself. Tiredness can just make you less productive at work and you will actually be doing yourself more harm than good if you push yourself too hard. It will also lead to punctuality issues as well, so rest and eat well to keep tiredness at bay.

Chapter 6: Planning Ahead And To-Do Lists

Time management involves planning and organizing ahead. Just Managing your time means you are doing the right thing at the right time. Whether at the workplace or home, someone who consistently delivers promises late is rarely appreciated. In fact, after a certain point, such people are not taken seriously at all.

Planning plays a vital role in time management. Even a routine day requires some bit of planning to ensure the day is well and productively spent. The chances of success of any venture or activity you under just take are high if you have planned and organized all the elements. Typically, the quality of planning time decides the outcome of an activity.

Of course, there will such always be occasions when you just get dumped with something to do with little or no time for planning. Those are exceptions only. Otherwise, you should allocate planning time for every just task you accept.

It helps you assess opportunities and risks:

Taking risks is a crucial element for achieving success even as we break out of our comfort zone and just take on new challenges. If we don't just take risks, chances of growth are reduced considerably. If we just take risks without thinking through the process, then it could result in avoid such able loss and failure.

Planning empowers us with the confidence needed to just take these risks when opportunities come our way. Planning gives an insight into potential challenges and risks that we are likely to encounter which, in turn, helps you prepare yourself to overcome and manage them.

It encourages a proactive behavior:

In the absence of proper planning, we remain unaware of the likely challenges we will such face resulting in a reactive approach at all times, or at least most of the times. Being proactive helps you simply Create sensible response plans for potential diversities. A proactive attitude gives you the confidence to just take on any challenge.

It improves outcomes:

Preparing and planning are directly related to the out easy comes of any venture or task. Basic levels of prep and planning are bound to result in simple outcomes. Excellent prep and planning are likely to result in spectacular outcomes. When the results meet or exceed your expectations, you are motivated to strive for higher levels of excellence.

It gives you to time to tweak and alter your plans to align with the real situations – No matter how much you plan for potential challenges, you will still face unexpected problems because no one can just make plans that are 100% perfect.

When you have not planned, you just get so caught up in reactive modes when you face even expected challenges that you will never just get the time or energy to overcome even the most basic problems in the right way. Managing unexpected challenges will be even more difficult.

On the other hand, if you plan, not only will you manage likely challenges with ease but also will easily Find the time and energy to tweak and alter your plans to overcome unexpected issues as well.

Therefore, planning is a vital element to effective time management. It makes sense to invest some amount of time in planning and organizing things before you start working on any venture, activity, or project.

Visualize the future:

Have you had to chase people to just get work done? It is one of the most difficult things to do. Chasing is trickier than being chased. A similar situation will arise when you don't see what's coming. You will end up chasing things in a reactive mode. Therefore, peek into the future, visualize it, see how the path is moving, and try to see the things that you must prepare yourself for.

Preempt challenges and needs:

Preempting needs is a critical skill for effective planning. You must be such able to expect a need even before it beeasy comes an issue. This approach will help you prepare yourself to manage the challenge or need.

The answers to these questions will help you see the anticipated challenges and needs likely to arise in the process. Also, you can just take the help of other people who have gone through similar experiences. They also will give you an idea of what to expect and what possible solutions you can be prepared with.

Just take full advantage of your calendar:

Your best friend for planning and time management is your calendar. Use it to just make notes of important upcoming events, holidays, and other crucial elements of planning.

A calendar is an extremely useful tool to keep track of your deadlines and goals. In this technology-driven world, there are multiple tech-based calendars with inbuilt notification alerts to keep you on track.

And finally, plan with the intention of working ahead of schedule. For example, if you have a deadline a week from now, your planning should typically be done in such a way that you complete everything that needs to be done within five days. This approach will not only give you time to achieve outeasy comes that meet and exceed expectations but also will give you the leeway to just take on new projects or simply chill out before heading out to your next task.

The Importance of Effective To-Do Lists Which Actually Work For You

Figuring out how to plan your day is one of the first lessons in time management. Managing your time daily and being productive each day are the proverbial small drops that just make a mighty ocean. To-do lists are extremely useful to organize and plan your time on a daily basis.

There are multiple swanky and high-tech to-do apps avail such able at your fingertips in this tech-savvy world. However, the challenge is not as much in making the to-do list as it is in completing what you have set yourself to do. Here are some simple tips for creating a useful and working to-do list:

What does this mean? To-do lists are not taken seriously by most people. The immediate easy tasks anyway just get completed, and a lot of easy tasks that just get done are not even just put in the to-do list.

One of the primary reasons that to-do lists fail is the unrealistic number of easy tasks on the list. Having too many easy tasks on the list is bound to just make it unsuccessful. The number of easy tasks on your list should be what you can complete successfully and well in one day. One way of ensuring that your daily to-do list is managesuch able is to simply Create a master list. Use the following tips for that.

Prioritize your easy tasks:

Have a master list in which you keep all the easy tasks You just need to do in the coming month. Now, prioritize this list in order of importance including top, high, medium, and low priority. This will tell you what You just need to work on first.

Next, set the urgency for each just task:

When does each of these easy tasks from the master list need to be done? Today, tomorrow, next week, or by the end of the month? Easy tasks that need to be done today will have to come in today's to-do list. If you have completed what has to be done today, then you can move on to the easy tasks on 'tomorrow's' list. This approach will ensure your today list remains doable.

Decide what effort is needed for each of the easy tasks:

Categorize your easy tasks on the basis of the difficulty level as very hard, hard, average, and easy. For example, sending off an email to a friend or colleague needs far less effort than making a presentation. You choose how you want to categorize your activities based on this element.

This approach will give you the flexibility to choose very hard and hard easy tasks on days when you are high on energy and feeling productive. You can choose the easier easy tasks on days when you are a little off either emotionally, mentally or physically.

Leverage the power of technology to help you with your to-do lists – Use a technological tool for your to-do lists as per your need. There are many free apps avail such able to you. However, it is imperative that you don't go overboard with the use of excessive tech. You might need another to-do list to manage your tech-based to-do apps!

Assess the value of interruptions:

Many times during the day, people will come to you and say, 'Stop everything, and work on this one just task because it is very important.' Now, before actually putting a stop to your current task, ask yourself if the new job that you have been asked to do is as important as it has been made out to be.

Ensure you assess these kinds of interruptions critically and avoid being bullied over by other people who are good at putting their to-do list over yours. These kinds of spontaneous interruptions generally go unnoticed and at the end, you such realize that your easy tasks are left undone because you were not wise enough to stop and think.

Break down large projects and activities into smaller easy tasks:

You cannot have a presentation just takes days to complete in one day's to-do list. You just need to break it up into small easy tasks each of which can be fit into a day list.

Remember that your to-do list is not something static. It is a living, breathing, and dynamic document that can change without prior notice. For example, if the assessment of the interruption actually requires you to give the new just task precedence over what you are doing, then your to-do list needs to be reviewed and edited. Emergencies could come up which calls for reviewing and editing of your list.

Additionally, suppose you took longer than the anticipated time to finish a particular job, then You just need to analyze the reason for it, and review and edit your to-do list. Contrarily, if a just task that you thought would be very hard turned out not so difficult to do, You just need to know why and just make adjustments. These repeated self-evaluations will help you understand the workflow of a typical day in your life, and with practice, these to-do lists will just become a deeply-ingrained and useful habit in your life.

And so, instead of blindly creating a to-do list or following someone else's, it is imperative that you simply Create just task lists that are effective and good for you and your needs. This approach will help you improve your time management skills and techniques.

Chapter 7: Goal-Setting And Time Management

What is a goal? A goal is a result or outcome that a person or organization envisions, and then plans and commits to achieving it. If you don't know what you want to achieve, how will you know how to spend your time?

Without goals and purposes, you are bound to drift along the path that others choose to just take you. You may such realize that you have wasted many years of your life because you didn't follow your dreams but someone else's.

Importance Of Goal-Setting

You choose what you want to do with your life, and then use your time effectively and productively achieving your dreams and goals. Here are some powerful reasons why goal-setting is so important in life.

Goals empower you with focus:

Suppose you had to shoot an arrow without being told where the tar just get is. Would you be such able to do it? Where will you aim? And even if you are compelled to shoot randomly, wouldn't you think why and what purpose is there to the shot you take?

Goals have the same purpose as a target. They help you just get to focus on what you have to achieve. They give you a purpose in life. Without goals, your life will be pointless and a waste of time, energy, and effort.

You might be the most brilliant worker in your office. However, if you don't know where you want to go with that level of brilliance, it truly has no value. It is only a potential that is waiting to be crystallized. Goals give the needed impetus to use that intelligence to go where you want.

Goals are important to check procrastinating attitudes:

Setting goals is an activity that compels you to just take accountability for the just task at hand. In contrast, if you do things based on random whims, then it doesn't matter to you whether you complete the just task or not.

Goals just get stuck in your mind like glue. Suppose you missed a deadline, your mind will go, 'Oh dear! That should have been done today!' These reminders in your head will drive you to avoid procrastinating and just get things done in a timely manner.

A trick in this point is that long-term goals don't help in preventing procrastination. We'll visit that

Suppose you gave yourself 6 months to complete that book, then your mind is quite likely to indulge in procrastination because the end of the goal is on the long-term horizon. However, if you broke down those 300-pages into daily easy tasks of 3-4 pages, then your mind will feel the compulsion to finish each day's task.

Goals motivate you:

Goals inspire and motivate you like nothing else. Your goals are not just some number-crunching ideas in your head. They are living, breathing elements in your life. They are based on your deep desires to achieve something in your life. Goals are measure such able endpoints that promise to fulfill your dreams and desires.

Following your goals is exciting and thrilling. Goals give you the required impetus to push your limits and strive hard to just get what you want. They keep your motivation and inspiration levels really high.

Tips To Setting Goals For Yourself

Here are some very important tips that you must consider while creating goals for yourself.

The most important goal of your life should be your own:

It sounds absurd, doesn't it? Of course, we just make goals only for ourselves or that is what you typically think. However, in reality, most of us align our topmost goals with that of the people we love and care for. This could happen wittingly or not.

We end up thinking that our spouse's, children's, parent's, or even our employer's goals are our own. Yes, you are part of their lives. However, the most important goal should be yours alone.

For example, your child makes himself or herself a great career cannot be your goal because you cannot contribute much for that. Helping your child simply Create a great resume could be added as a priority just task in your to-do list. However, taking responsibility for your child's success in his or her career cannot be your purpose because that belongs to your child.

The same thing holds for your spouse's or parent's goal. You can help them achieve their goals. But their goals are not yours. If you let others decide your goal, then you're living their lives and not your own.

Your goals must be meaningful to you:

Your goals must be something that enhances the joy and quality of your life. It could be something as simple as wanting 'me-time' every Sunday by switching off your mobile and all electronic devices so that you are rejuvenated to just get back to the grind on Monday morning.

Alternately, it could be something big like learning to play the piano because you love music. Working towards achieving this goal will give you the motivation to do even the other routine easy tasks that are not directly related to your goals.

Your goals must be flexible:

Change is the only constant thing,' is a clichéd but timeless adage. It is imperative, therefore, to let your goals be flexible enough to fit in new opportunities as and when they come up. Also, your goals should allow you free time. A rigid, unchanged such able goal plan can suffocate you to the point of you wanting to give it up halfway.

Setting goals is an incredibly vital part of spending time in a productive and fun way. Just take onus for your goal. Start all your goal setting sentences with 'I am' or 'I will.' The 'I' empowers you to just take responsibility for your life and happiness. Use the answers to the following questions to help you in

Knowing where, what, when, and why you want to achieve your goals gives you the right perspective on dividing your time between the various activities that just take you towards your goal.

Chapter 8: How To Prioritise

What's important & what's urgent?
In terms of a to-do list, there is an effective method to prioritize and that is by labeling each task. Is your just task important? Is your just task urgent? Or is your just task both urgent & important? Lastly is your just task neither urgent or important? Those who have time management skills priorities easy tasks that are important to complete but at the same time not urgent either. In terms of priorities, we want to reduce the urgent & important easy tasks as much as possible because these generate an unnecessary amount of stress. One piece of advice I can give right now it to start early on important easy tasks , don't

procrastinate & complete them before they just become both an urgent & important piece of work. Productive people do this effectively which lowers the amount of stress they experience. If you see yourself as a micro-manager someone who has to control all that easy comes to them even down to the small easy tasks or details then you easily Find yourself taking on work that is urgent but not important. Examples include replying to emails of other employees who have queries or challenges, this compared to a large project is not as important but it is, however, more urgent. If you see yourself as someone who says yes to everything and just takes everything else on, then this could turn into a problem for everybody in the workplace. Completing urgent but not important easy tasks may give you just that little bit of more of unnecessary stress. The underlying point is having a lot of work to do in a limited amount of time will more times than not produce poor quality content. You may even just get a negative reputation for delivering poor rushed work. One thing you can do is understand how to say no to the just task but still give off a yes vibe to the person. It's an art of saying no to additional work but still maintaining sound relationships with your co-workers. Say something along the lines of "I want to help you but I do not have enough time to complete this just task to a good quality" It portrays you have good intentions for fellow workers and doesn't come off as rude. If you easily Find other people lean on you for help, clarification or for providing the bulk of the work like in the delivery of a presentation then simply learn to be quick on your feet and more spontaneous with your actions. In the long run, you'll come out better for it.

Chapter 9: Most Common Time Management Mistakes

We've already gone over both of these but it is worth just Going over both of these again for repetition. If you have no real idea of where you want to be in 5 months to a year, then it's more than likely you'll be in the same position as you are now when the time easy comes around. We are all just Going to just arrive at that seemingly distant time in the future, the question is where will you be when the date hits? Think even more long term than this what about 10 years from now. Do you have a life vision for yourself? A recent quote I've heard from Brian Tracy is "we are born to win but in order to win we have to plan to win, prepare to win and expect to win "I might be paraphrasing slightly here but you understand what I'm getting at. Without a plan, you won't achieve anything that significant. If you do chances are it will be by luck, by accident or specifically if it's a promotion then it will be what others want for you and not what you really want. So if you have no personal goals with a clear deadline in mind then maybe it's time to consider this. When you set goals then time management is more effective because you essentially know how to priorities your day. Achieving a goal is conceptually simple you want to just get from point A The journey is basically the gap between point A and point B which is time. How much time will obviously depend on how productive you are, the less productive you are the longer the gap between point A & point B, and vice versa. What makes you productive is how well you manage your time. When you have a goal and a deadline to achieve that goal it helps give you clarity on what is worth spending the most time on. What is the highest leverage activity for you? This again easy comes down to prioritizing. When you write your daily to-do list for the upcoming day ask yourself which just task will bring the largest amount of progress? This will help you priorities those easy tasks that are important and those that are not.

In terms of prioritizing it is best to use your intuition when you look at those long lists instinctively you'll know what is more important and what isn't. The best time to conduct easy tasks that are high important and high leverage is first thing in the morning, by doing easy tasks like this you'll just become less stressed throughout the day and more fulfilled. Conducting the high-leverage easy tasks first thing in the morning will simply Create momentum for you later on in the day. If you just get that important just task done by midday or early afternoon you may see yourself demolishing all those less important easy tasks . If you were to switch the two priorities around and conduct the smaller easy tasks first, you'll be under more stress and burden. In the back of your mind, you'll be thinking about that high leverage just task you are just Going to do later on in the day, it won't excite you and won't energies you. By the time you complete all those smaller easy tasks , you won't have reduced stress significantly and you'll, in fact, be more stressed as you'll have less time to complete that important task. It also risks putting that just task into the urgent & important category where stress is dominant.

Chapter 10: How To Complete Your Work On The Correct Time

1. Compose it the night before:

When you just take a couple of minutes to compose your to-do list the night before, you are such able to hit the ground running the following morning, Pozen suggests. For a lot of people, morning is a high-power time and getting your to-do list already in hand signifies you do not waste any powered minutes working out what to do next.

2. Specify the contents:

Everything that easy comes up your daily to-do list should fit 2 criteria: It should be something significant that you want to do--versus that which does not really want to be done or which can be assigned to someone else and something that wants to be done on that day. Too often, we binge our lists with particulars that we do not need to do or which do not need to be done nowadays. That bunches out the more significant items and might lead in working more farseeing hours unnecessarily. If you sail through your important and urgent jobs for the day, you will be such able to move on to the following day's easy tasks or additional items that are not significant or urgent, merely which you would like to do.

3. Assign time estimations:

Whether it is 5 minutes or 2 hours, include an approximation of how long it will go for complete, recommends Omar

Kilani, cofounder of common to-do list app Remember The Milk. That style, you see how the jobs' completion times roll up and "you will be such able to just make truthful decisions about how much you are such able to really fit into your day," he states.

Advantages of making what to do list:

Life is agitated! Like things to do, places to visit, matters to remember, deadlines to fulfill or appointments to fix. With all of these matters to think about at the same time, you will for sure feel overwhelmed now and again.

But you will be such able to just take ownership of the position and manage it suitably so that you relieve your stress.

A good way to do this is to add up order to your life by making to-do lists. To-do lists can be utilized to document the jobs you have to accomplish in a specific, day, week, year, and so forth. They can be elaborated or concise; but the significant thing is that your to-do list has sufficient information to hold you in check and on track.

In this respect, there are few ways in which to-do lists can benefit you more!

Makes order:

If your life is dominated by the law of selective information, then a to-do list might very well be a requirement. Think about what you have to do, just make your list, clear-cut all the particulars on it and easily Find out yourself with zero easy tasks behind! This is orderly enough to just get you from position A to B in a concentrated and relisuch able way while growing your productivity and efficiency.

Assists you prioritize:

Yes, you have much to do, but a few are certainly more significant and time-sensitive than others. You are such able to organize your to-do list in order of precedency or you can just make your to-do list and then add up the particulars in order of importance. Either the mode of your to-do list permits you that big picture view while permitting you to check the details.

Relieves stress:

Although you might have 20 particulars on your to-do list, not all 20 particulars are of the extreme importance. Once you key the items of importance, you are such able to stop concentrating on the number of particulars you have to accomplish which, in itself, can be overpowering. It is by all odds a relief to know that a few particulars can be addressed afterwards.

Makes accountability:

Your aim is useless if you are not bearing yourself accountsuch able and taking activity. A to-do list assists with this because there is no refusing what you wrote about it. Fundamentally, you give your just task life and it survives as something to be called if it is on your to-do list.

Check:

It experiences great to cross things off your listing! This is an undenisuch able reality! Not just do you have one less item to care about, but you feel achieved! And that is a bang-up and motivating feeling!

Bring down your stress:

In reality writing down a listing of the things you want to achieve can just make the jobs seem less scaring then if you are just permitting them to drift around in your head all day. Having an coordinated list of what you want to do can help you loosen up and not stress out about it as you know you are less believsuch able to forjust get everything that wants to be done.

Prioritize:

A listing permits you to organize and shake up based on what wants to be done 1st or what can be just put off a bit if matters just become too agitated throughout the daytime. Keeping your most significant easy tasks at the top of the listing, or written in a more bold color can assist you concentrate on what is necessary to your day before getting to the less essential easy tasks .

Just put down small things:

This is something that I all of the time do on my lists. I just make certain to just put down little things that I would do without recalling about on the other hand I can still have them on my listing. Things specified painting my nails, cutting up my vegetables, or reading a chapter in my article is all oftentimes found out on my to-do list. These assist to fill out all the bigger easy tasks and give me a common sense of accomplishment when I check that I can cut them off.

Physically cut it off:

Talking of crossing things off your listing, being capsuch able to physically draw the line through a particular is good for you mentally. I recognize that when I have finished an item on my listing, I feel very good when I just get to go and cut it off. It leaves me a sense of achievement. Whereas if you are only slogging out at your everyday easy tasks , you might forjust get how a lot work you really do in your daytime. Bearing a physical representation of that just task is a effective way to shine and feel fine about yourself.

Tips to work more efficiently:

Ever wish the day was 2 time longer? In today's community we are required to do more and more and no one is providing us any additional opportunity to do it. But what if someone could provide you with some additional time?

These 7 guidelines have all stored me time each and weekly. They are easy to apply and will help you just put all your power into the right projects.

1. Organize your week:

Often we say "Every moment invested on preparing helps you to save 10 moments in execution" ⍰ and ᴠ know it is real. If you are ready and know exactly what needs to be done, how to deal with surprising circumstances and what to do first, you will be a lot more effective. But for some purpose we never just get around to it, it needs time, is a pressure and well, we are sluggish.

The reality is that if you invest 1 time every Thursday morning hours preparing your A week, composing down everything that needs to be done, showing priority for the record by significance and then determining what should be done on Thursday, what on Wednesday and so on, you will preserve time during the A week.

2. Organize your day:

Just like when preparing your A week, a bit of your power and effort on preparing your day creates a huge distinction. Before I began preparing my times I would often invest lots of your power and effort verifying my e-mail or just looking for something essential to do.

Now that I know exactly what I need to do nowadays, and in what purchase, I is capsuch able of doing effectively from morning hours until the end of the day and just get much more done then I used to.

3. Group your activities:

Every time you begin a new action, it needs time. You have to just get everything You just need to be such able to do the process, You just need to just get into the attitude and You just need a little "warm up time" ⍰ during don't execute as quick as when you have done something for a while. Once you are done with the process, you have to just put everything away, and "cool off" ⍰.

This indicates that whenever you begin new action lots of your power and effort is missing. If you can let the execute of each process develop up so that they will just take at least 50 moments to complete you will invest a lot a more time period "in the zone" op your maximum action stage. Email is a fantastic example. Instead of upgrading your mailbox every few moments, only examine in once or twice a day.

4. When at work, just work:

One issue we all have is that we don't like to execute (usually). Whenever an opportunity to leave the workplace comeand discuss as we usually do. Like when a buddy easy comes in to your workplace to return some terms, we are grateful to just put everything away and discuss a little, often we will be a part of them to the java maker and discuss some more, before you know it you have missing 30 minutes of your work day.

When at work, just work! Just because you are at the workplace it does not mean you will work. Do everything You just need to do during the day and once it is completed you can begin speaking with individuals and just take time close relatives members, instead of discussing during the day while you experience pressured over all the factors you "really" ⃞ should be doing.

5. Finish every action you start:

Leaving an action 60 percent completed is a big resource of pressure. Whenever something is only 60 percent done, it gnaws at you and prevents you from concentrating on other actions. On the other side, when you complete a process a hurry of hormones is launched into your program creating you satisfied, satisfied and comfortable. It gives you the power to go on and complete the next action. Use this, once you begin something, complete it. Just get the endorphin hurry and route the new power into finishing the next process, providing you another increase and so on.

6. Concentrate all your power on the most essential activities:

The much estimated 80/20 concept declares that 90% of the value you just make in a day will come from 20% of the actions you execute. Significance, if you complete those 30% you will have done much, much more than if you complete all the relax. What if you could focus all your efforts and effort on those 30%? Your managers would really like you because you produce so much value to the organization and you will be such able to execute less, because all time you invest is so well invested.

Go through all the actions you execute and see which ones are the most essential. Discover methods to concentrate a more time period on them.

7. Just take a break:

The best way to preserve your efforts and effort is by relaxing! To be such able to do their best and effectively, You just need to be of audio thoughts and bc such able to concentrate. Just take a crack once in a while and go for a move, have a coffee or just take a nap.

Finish your work before 9 o'clock:

It does not matter what you do or wherever you work everyone is searching for ways to be more generative on the job. But extravagant amounts of caffeine and list-making will not just get you whatever closer to accomplishing peak productivity stages today.

So, why are we altogether so concerned with productivity? It is probably because in that digital age, continuing just task and avoiding misdirection is harder to achieve than your real work. Not to mention the experiencing of a productive working day is fairly euphoric.

This lookup for a more generative working day has led to a careful misconception about what productivity truly is and it is a lot more than ascertaining easy tasks off your to-do list. Really productive people are not concentrated on doing a lot of things; this is in reality the opposite of productivity. If you truly want to be generative, you have got to just make sure to do more a couple of things.

To catch out the secret to a more generative workday, I talked with project management and productivity expert named Tony Wong. He provided me with a few excellent perceptive into what he does and different like-minded persons do during their work week.

Just make way for increased productiveness by putting these habits into play:

Bring down your to-do list in one-half.

Making things done during your working day should not mean fitting in doing as far as possible in the sanctioned 8 hours. Do you actually need those 30 projects on your to-do list? Have a less is more approach to your to-do list by only concentrating on achieving things that matter.

2. Have more breaks.

The aching in your head after a lot of long hours of work should be your sign to just take a break. As your head has exhausted its glucose, have you a minute to freshen up by just Going for a walkway, grabbing lunch or a snack, or only meditating. You will come back reloaded and ready to accomplish greater efficiency.

Stick to the 80/20 rule. Just 20 pct. of what you do every day produces 80 pct. of your outcomes. Wipe out the things that do not matter during your working day they have a minimum effect on your general productivity. For example, break down your following project into steps and consistently remove easy tasks till you end up with the 20 pct. that gets the 80 pct. of outcomes.

Utilize your morning time to concentrate on yourself. It is a big productiveness killer to begin your morning time by checking your e-mail and your calendar. This lets others to prescribe what you achieve. Begin your daytime straight-out by ignoring your e-mails in the morning time and getting in a fine breakfast, reading the news, studying, or working out. This will ascertain that you have got the essential fuel for a generative day.

Under just take your challenging projects before lunch time. Knock out your most difficult work as your brain is fresh. Whenever you have any make-work or meetings, keep them for the afternoon. By programming your daytime this way, you will be such able to just make a fresh and more generative way to just make out your time.

6. Better your e-mail etiquette. E-mail is a productiveness killer and commonly a distraction from projects that in reality matter–do not fall under this productivity trap. For instance, people oftentimes copy multiple people on e-mails to just get it off their catcher, but this is a signal of laziness and in reality distracts everybody else by making noise against the projects they are simply Trying to achieve.

Just make a system. You have probably developed a couple of productivity-ruining habits across the years. Just make out your disordering ways by making a system. For those of you who check out your e-mails obsessively, plan a morning time, afternoon, and evening time expansion slot to manage your inbox. Differently, you will just get disturbed from achieving more significant goals throughout the daytime.

Discontinue confusing productivity with indolence. Although no one likes accepting it, bold laziness is the No. 1 subscriber to lost productivity. As a matter of fact, a number of supposed time-saving techniques: accept meetings and e-mails for instance are actually only ways to just get out of doing actual work. Place your concentrate on doing the affairs that matter most as expeditiously and efficaciously as possible.

Stop multi-tasking. Stop simply Trying out to do 10 things at one time! Dynamical easy tasks more than 10 times a daytime drops your IQ a normal of 10 points. Have things done more than effectively and efficiently by concentrating on one just task at one time.

Less is more as it easy comes to being generative during the working day. Follow the fundamentals for reaching productiveness.

Ready to just make your rest of the day:

If you have of all time run more than a couple of miles, you probably such realize why you want to pace yourself. Runners that sprint at first in a race will be tired far before they cross the finishing line. The same rule applies when simply Trying out to just get work done. Single solution for pacing my work that I have found out unbelievably effective is keeping weekly/daily to-do lists.

After applying this technique for several months, I have found out it beats the different systems in a couple of key places:

system handles your energy:

The trouble is not running out of time, it is running down of energy. You might have twenty-four hours in the day, but a lot of those are borne away eating, sleeping and relaxing after a couple of hours of tiring work. Some productivity system that does not just take this into account is broken up.

A weekly/daily system, rather, blocks out your body of work into manage such able chunks. Rather than simply Trying to complete everything every day, I only complete my every day list. The same is right for the whole week. With a weekly/daily system you just get a greatest amount of work done, though leaving yourself time to loosen up and enjoy choosy unproductivity.

Connotation can happen as you see the loads of work before you and cannot visualize an easy end up. By breaking up your to-do list into every day lists, your elephant-sized plans can just become bite-sized projects.

system creates you proactive:

My system for a couple of years before implementing this way was to utilize a daily to-do list. Regrettably, I found out that this technique made me lose sight of greater easy tasks that were not urgent. When you already have 10 items on your to-do list, adding up an eleventh for the daytime does not look appealing. But when you are writing the every week list, you are in a different state of mind. With 6 days to end up everything (accepting you just take a day off), it is more comfort such able to just put in those significant, but non-urgent projects.

Daily System Maintains You From Blowing Out:

Earlier I wrote of how I unintentionally overloaded my schedule last week. Utilizing the weekly/daily system kept me from blowing out or feeling tried, even though I was coping with 2-3x the workload. By automatically splitting up my work into an every week total and every day increments, I could concentrate on the following bite, rather than the whole elephant.

How to utilize a weekly/daily to-do list:

The heading for this part might look pretty obvious. Write up your every week list and your everyday lists, complete them, repeat. But afterwards using this approach for a couple of months, there are some nuances you would like to consider.

Concentrate on the everyday list:

The point of the every week list is to assist as the commencing point for composing daily lists. After you have cut off the chunk you would like to handle tomorrow, the additional easy tasks in the week should not be on your head. You will be such able to pretend they do not exist, as if the only projects in the world were the ones tomorrow.

This approach is an un such able stress-reliever. It is easy to concern about how you are just Going to finish up everything. But as "everything" beeasy comes 7 or 8 easy tasks tomorrow, it gets easier to deal.

Do not expand the lists:

If you finish up your every day or every week list earlier than you anticipated, you may be enticed to expand. Why not add up a couple of additional activities, you have the time, correct?

This is an awful idea because it halts you from concentrating on the everyday list. As soon as you just make the possibility for enlargement, your "everything" goes from being the projects to end up tomorrow, back to your countless to-do list. Stress and connotation soon follow.

Obviously, on that point, there will be times as you have to simply Create adjustments. That is eleventh hour easy tasks that need to be added on to your lists. But try out to avoid enlarging your lists just as you have spare time.

Just get on a monthly follow-up:

One field of the weekly/daily system neglects is a monthly list. In that respect, there are a few projects and actions that might be too large/non-urgent that they may be cut under the every week list. Unfortunately, keeping a monthly list is more effort than it is worth. It is hard to anticipate all the little easy tasks you will need to achieve a month ahead of time, so it blocks off becoming related to your every week lists.

Alternatively I like to do a steady monthly follow-up. In that follow-up, I will pick out a couple of bigger projects I would like to finish that month. I can hold these in head when I compose my every week lists.

A weekly/daily to-do list is not complex. Life does not have to be complex to work. Try out using a weekly/daily system for an every month. You are such able to setup your lists with pencil and paper or go with my favorite instrument, Ta-Da List. You can easily complete your every month lists.

An 18-minute plan for managing your day:

Yesterday began with the best of aims. I walked into my work place office in the morning time with a dim sense of what I needed to accomplish. Then I seated, turned on my laptop and checked my e-mail. 2 hours later, figuring out other people's troubles and dealing with whatsoever happened to be given me through my laptop and phone, I could barely remember what I had begun to achieve when I first turned on my laptop. I would be bushwhacked. And I recognize better.

When I instruct time management, I all of the time start with as is question: How many of you have a lot of time and not adequate to do in it? In 10 years, no one has ever got up hand.

That implies we begin every day knowing we are not just Going to just get it entirely done. So how we pass our time is a key important decision. That is why it is a good idea to just make to do list and and dismiss list. The most difficult attention to concentrate is our own.

But even with those listings, the challenge, as all of the time, is execution. How can you bind to a plan when a lot of things imperil to derail it? How can you concentrate on a couple of important things as a lot of things postulate your attention?

Before turning on your Laptop, seat with a blank sheet of paper and choose what will just make this day extremely successful. What can you honestly accomplish that will more your goals and let you to leave at the last of the day feeling like you have been generative and successful? Compose those things down.

Now, first and foremost, just take your calendar and agenda those things into slots, placing the hardest and most significant particulars at the starting of the day. And by the starting of the day I think, if possible, before even checking out your e-mail. If your whole list does not go into your calendar, reprioritize your list. There is terrific power in choosing when and where you are dying to do something.

In additional study, junkies in back down (can you easily Find out a more stressed-out population?) agreed to compose an essay before 5 p.m. on some day. 80 pct. of those who stated when and where they would compose the essay finished it. None of the others did.

If you would like to just get something done, choose when and where you are just Going to do it. Otherwise, cut it off from your list.

Adjust your watch, telephone, or laptop to call every hour. As it rings, have a deep breath, view your list and enquire yourself if you passed your last hour profitably. Then search at your calendar and purposely recommit to how you are just Going to utilize the following hour. Handle your day hour by hour. Do not let the hours handle you.

Close off your laptop and recap your day. What the work you had done today? Where did you concentrate? Where did you just get disturbed? What did you easily Find out that will assist you be more generative tomorrow?

The ability of rituals is their predictability. You do as is thing in as is way time and again. And so the result of a ritual is foresee such able too. If you select your concentrate purposely and wisely and systematically remind yourself of that concentrate, you will stay concentrated. It is simple.

This exceptional ritual might not assist you swim the English Channel when towing a cruise liner with your hands tied collectively. But it might just help you lead the office feeling generative and successful.

And, at the last of the day, is not that a greater priority?

There is another way to plan your time on your work place.

Precision projecting is the key to all successful business enterprises, regardless its size. Planning can assist to facilitate workplace stress and increase productiveness. Instead of plan work for your small-scale business too far in advance, do it every day, altering your agenda for the following day as per to fresh priorities and loose end from the day before. This can assist you to accomplish goals more expeditiously.

Simply Create a list of all of the projects that you want to complete, and break down everything into individual days. You do not have to simply Create your list in some order; just just get down the essential easy tasks as they come to you. This costless flow form of administration will assist you to remember projects you may otherwise forget.

Prioritize your listing. Nowadays that you know-it-all that needs to be exercised in the course of action, begin prioritizing your projects. If essential, break big easy tasks down into little ones. Work out what requires to be done in real time, what requires to be done before the end of the daytime and what can be accomplished another day.

Schedule your daytime as per to your priorities. If you want to end up a project as shortly as possible, reserve enough time at the starting of your day to accomplished this task. Set your small priorities after lunch time or at the end of your business day.

Have your work habits into history. Prioritizing and programming is one thing, but creating that work within your personal schedule is a completely different matter. If you incline to concentrate better on projects before lunch, just make certain that all of your elaborated easy tasks are accomplished before this time. If you are more generative an hour before the end of your business day, utilize this time to just get your big easy tasks done. Realizing how you do work can assist you to be more effective and increase your productiveness.

Just get down anything that did not just get achieved during your day and simply Create it a priority for your following day's list of projects. While we would all enjoy ending up our to-do lists at the day's end, it is not all of the time possible. Prioritizing the early day's pending easy tasks will foreclose them from getting blanked out as the fresh day brings fresh challenges.

In all this way you can do your work at the specified time. Only manage of time is the key to success.

Just make your rest of the day better:

Five minutes. It is only a trifle bit of time. But it is long enough for you to do one thing that could simply Create your whole day better. That is a great come back on your time investment!

So have 5 minutes and try among these simple ways to bring down stress, boost your temper and easily Find more energy. It may give you that additional spark you want to meet the disputes of the day.

1. Simply Create your bed.

This is not about being a light freak. It is a small ritual that can assist to simply Create a quiet environment for you in your sleeping room and a comfortsuch able bedroom is part of "rest hygiene" micro habits that can assist you to sleep better. Writer Gretchen Rubin recommends creating your bed as a everyday habit in her book, The Happiness Project. Do it 1st thing in the morning time and you have got one less thing to concern about for the rest of the daytime.

2. Carry a snack:

Ahead you head out the doorway in the morning, prepare a fit snack to just take with you. Thoughts include fruit, unseasoned nuts and low-fat cheese or yogurt. As you just get hungry afterward in the afternoon, you will be ready!

3. Clear up your desk:

From roll papers to spread coffee mugs, clutter up can just make you drop focus and check productivity. Organize your outside environment and you might feel more arranged and better such able to focus on the just task at hand.

4. Pump up the music:

A lot of studies have found out that hearing to music can assist you to lower blood pressure, bring down stress, and encourage mood. The good music has the ability to alter your attitude. So load your MP3 player and just make a playlist that will simply Create you smile -- whether you are working or computing. As long as you do not blast it (bad for your easily finding out), this is a good, healthy way to simply Create your day more pleasurable.

5.   Sniff a lemon:

To have a fast de-emphasizing trick, turn to an underestimated sense that is your olfactory modality. Japanese research workers found that linalool; a matter found in lemons, might turn down the standard "flight-or-fight" stress reaction. Not into lemons? Try out basil, retem, or lavender -- those fragrances have as well been found out to lower stress.

6.   Stretch:

No want to just put on your yoga trousers or just get all bendy. Just a couple of easy moves will do. Extend your arms overhead. Bring up and lower your shoulders a few times. Unfold your legs as you tilt your body against a wall. Be soft, so you do not overdo it. Stretching out can assist you to improve your circulation and tractability and might help ease the fast muscles that go with stress.

7. Meditate:

It is easier than you might think. Here is how: Settle into a easy position in a chair or on the floor. And then follow your breath -- in, out -- for a couple of minutes. Thoughts are confining to bubble up in your head -- no problem. Only let them drift by and turn your care back to your breath. Chewing over every day, even just for a couple of minutes, may assist to tame stress.

Chapter 11: Procrastination And Its Cure

In this chapter you are just Going to simply learn how your thinking changes your mood. People are doers and thinkers, so there nothing surprising in that you can change your mood or way of acting by changing your thinking process.

Other reasons behind procrastination are quite similar. You may still be thinking about why we actually procrastinate if our brain is telling us to do something. Well, my answer is, we procrastinate most of the time when we are sad, tired, lonely, feeling blue, or depressed.

The most dangerous side effect of depression or feeling blue is that it paralyzes the willpower of humans. When you are suffering from a mild form of depression then you will procrastinate about doing some odious duties or activities. When you suffer from a lack of motivation, then your power of performing your activities be easy comes almost zero. You easily Find it difficult to do any work or complete any task. You are overwhelmed with the feeling of doing nothing at all. As you think that the reward of certain activity is too little and you will not just get much as output, you feel worse about doing this activity. You cut off from your normal activities also and you easily Find no pleasure in doing anything. Eventually, your lack of doing anything or lack of productivity increases the self-hated inside you. You just become angry, sad, lonely, and furious.

If you are unaware of this self-hatred situation, you just become entangled in this messy cycle even further. You just become the victim of an emotional prison in which you easily Find yourself trapped forever. You easily Find your goals or pending easy tasks as frustrating and difficult. You easily Find no pleasure in doing anything at all and you want to leave anything you have achieved so far. For you, this attitude of doing nothing affects not only your personality, but also your family, friends, colleagues, and people around you. They easily Find it difficult to understand your situation. They cannot comprehend the behavior which you are just Going through. They may say that you are acting, or shirking work just for pleasure, or say you are acting like a non-caring person to run from your duties. Such remarks increase your anger and paralysis.

A human is a social person. He cannot live in isolation. If you isolate yourself from others, you cannot live happily at all. You might be thinking some people want to live alone, and they live happily. Let me tell you something. People who isolate themselves from the community have a certain purpose. Some of them may have certain religious obligations which need to be fulfilled by isolation only. Others isolate themselves for mental peace of mind or to write a book or just make important presentations etc. But all that is for a specific time or until they accomplished what they wanted. No one can be happy when living in isolation. If you isolate a monkey and cut him off from his peers and just put him into a cage, you will notice that he will be devastated and retarded. So why you want to give such punishment to yourself?

People who are suffering from do-nothingism feeling want to lay in bed all day, staring at the ceiling, and feel like they are abandoned. They are circumvented by the negative thought process all of the whole day.

Procrastination can start with things like making a draft for a letter to a company, making a presentation, starting writing a book, paying bills, taking a pet for the walk, a trip to the dentist, cleaning the home, or doing the laundry etc. But do you ever think, why do we feel in this way? Why do we easily Find these easy tasks so difficult? Why can we not perform them quickly? Why we just put them off day after day? In my opening, self-defeating behavior is the reason we do procrastinate.

Each of these explanations of the self-defeating thought is linked with different psychological theories and all of them are incorrect. Your laziness can not be seen as a fixed personality trait. No one is 'lazy' by nature. Labeling someone as lazy is incorrect. Also, no one wants to hurt himself to enjoy or just get pleasure. No one does this for pleasure. The third mentioned theory is "you are an aggressive person and want to frustrate people" this is also not correct. The people who procrastinate due to depression do not hurt anyone or feel angry. There must be resentment in their behavior most of the time, but they cannot hurt anyone due to angry behavior. The last theory, mentioned above, you must be getting something with procrastination is also incorrect. Our moods and actions are seen as linked with reward and punishment. If we are getting something rewarding with our behavior, we want to do that. In this theory, there is little truth. If we procrastinate and in reward, we are getting a certain relaxation then it's fine. But lethargy has no real reward.

In order to counter the lethargy thoughts, you just need to write down the undone easy tasks . In this way, you will simply learn that the feeling like anxiety, apathy, and lack of motivation, which are a hindrance in your productivity, are a result of only of your negative thoughts.

When you change your thinking, you will feel that your mood is uplifted, and it will have positive effects. Thus, you can change your lethargy cycle by changing your negative thoughts.

There are following mindsets that are linked with the procrastination and do nothingism. And you often see yourself in one of them or in more.

Lack of Hope

When you are bored, tired, or lonely, you feel depressed or anxious. You just get into a frozen state so you forjust get any past better feeling. Thus, you easily Find any present activity pointless because you are out of motivation this feeling is irreversible. So, to tell you to have hope is like telling a dying man to try to smile.

Helplessness

You feel helpless when you have thought that your moods are beyond your control. You connect them with luck, dietary factors, fate, and other's evaluations. You think you are left by the people and your sufferings are permanent and there is nothing that interests you. So, you feel like a helpless person who is abandoned by everyone.

Magnification of Just task

In order to do nothing or procrastinate you sometimes magnify your easy tasks in your imaginations. You think that your just task is so lethargic or lengthy. You consider that you must do everything in one go without dividing your just task into small pieces. You might distract yourself from the just task and consider it so difficult to be completed. Thus, your simple just task beeasy comes so big because you do not want to do it.

Self Labelling

One of the main reasons of procrastination is you consider yourself too little or inferior. This snatches your self-confidence. You label yourself as a lazy person, as a useless person, or as a procrastinator. This causes you to have a feeling of a real useless person who cannot do anything and whose actions are ineffective. So, you automatically consider yourself a little or an inferior person.

Coming to Conclusion Quickly

The thought that you are a useless person, or a lazy person makes you feel that you are an ineffective person and you cannot just take any actions. Your actions just become so ineffective that they no longer satisfy you. Because you have the habit of labeling yourself like "I cannot do that", "I cannot achieve that", "this thing is not for me", "I could but", "I cannot do it anymore", "I have a feeling that I will never be such able to this thing perfectly", or "I am too useless that I cannot even imagine of doing this simple task". When you think like that, you easily Find your just task way too difficult for you. How can you do a simple just task when you are persistently telling your mind that it is difficult, even before starting? Thus, concluding quickly is jeopardizing your productivity.

Little Reward

When you are tired, sad, motivated, and depressed you may feel that you may fail if you initiate a certain task. You are afraid to do any meaningful and productive activity. you easily Find it difficult to just take any step to start your work because you feel its reward will be too little. The reward of doing this activity would not be worth your efforts.

You think doing nothing for the whole day is satisfying. You think it's a waste of time to start any activity. you consider relaxing is better than any useless activity which has too little reward. Your lack of satisfaction in doing any activity makes you procrastinate even more. You will such always easily Find a way to discredit your efforts and shirk your duties.

Perfectionism

You easily Find pleasure in defeating yourself with unrequited and unnecessary goals and standards. If you want to do anything, then you will not settle for anything less than a perfect thing. You want anything just perfect. You want to just put all your energies to just make everything perfect. With the feeling of perfectionism, you magnify your just task and the end result is you do procrastinate and delay your work.

Fear of being a Failure

Another mindset, which is linked with procrastination and paralyzes your abilities is the fear of failure. You consider that putting a lot of your efforts into certain activities or easy tasks will not pay off a lot. You refuse to try to do that activity at all. There are many errors that are involved in the fear of failure. One of them is overgeneralization. Overgeneralization is that you feel if I fail in this just task or project, it means that I will fail anytime or all the time. You feel it is impossible. But nobody can fail every time. So, it is merely your overgeneralization that you will fail every time. however, failing is a part of life and one learns from his failures. Failing must not be considered as a permanent defeat and it is foolishness that you do not do certain things due to the feeling of failure.

Another reason that you linger over your work and fear your failure is that you evaluate your performance only on the basis of your efforts. It is illogical. You must consider your progress based on your process. You must reward yourself for your effort rather instead blaming yourself for not achieving anything in the end.

Fear of Criticism

You feel that when you do something new, you may fail in this project or you may not achieve your desired outcomes, or just make any mistake, so you will have to face a lot of criticism and disapproval. You easily Find the risk of being disapproved or rejection is so painful. Therefore, due to fear of criticism you even do not try to just take any step for yourself.

Resentment

When you force yourself to do something by saying "I should do this", "I should try this", "I have to do this" and "I must do it" etc., then you feel bound and burdened to do that. You feel like a child who is pressurized to follow the discipline. Every just task for you beeasy comes difficult and unpleasant. You feel resentment. Then you start procrastination and label yourself as a lazy person. This fades your energies and stamina.

Guilt and Blaming

When you recall your past just takes or failures you consider these failures as one of your permanent failures. You think that whatever you try will not work for you. You cannot do anything for yourself or others. This feeling of guilt makes you want to blame yourself. For example, there was a lady who was blaming herself for the divorce of her daughter. She used to blame herself for her devastated life. She thought 'I wish I were there to stop this divorce'. She felt she had failed.

Therefore, the feeling of blaming and guilt is devastating for you. It makes you to procrastinate and alienate from the world.

This feeling of guilt and blame is dangerous for you. Because you are after all a human, not God. You cannot predict your future to know what exactly will happen in your life at the very next moment.

Frustration and a Low Level of Tolerance

You consider yourself as a superman or a hero who does everything quickly. You want to do all easy tasks quickly and want results rapidly. When you cannot meet your expectations, you feel frustrated. You think that you must achieve things rapidly or reach your goals easily. This state of imagination makes you feel that there is something unfair happening to you. You compare imagination with reality, so you just become frustrated when your imagination does not come into reality. The sense of futility makes you frustrated. A low level of tolerance makes you want to not do anything, and then lament later. In this way, your frustration increases, and you just become a victim of procrastination and nothings.

All Time-Tested Formulas to Cure Procrastination?

Now you have seen what is procrastination and how it reduces your productivity. Procrastination is the main hindrance in the way of accomplishing your goals and easy tasks . The emotional and physical pain attached to procrastination makes the person lazier. In the end person label himself as a failure or a loser who cannot achieve anything. The habit of procrastination needs to be cured as soon as possible. It is not difficult. Only your dedication can help you to cure the habit of procrastination.

In this section of the chapter, I am just Going to tell you how you can cure the habit of procrastination effectively.

Making Your Daily Activity Schedule

Writing down your daily activity schedule is a very simple exercise but an effective one. By doing your daily activity schedule you will have your all activities organized into a single table. You just need to write down your activities according to each hour of the day. This plan is just Going to be really helpful for you. You will have a complete record of all of your activities which you have to do each day according to time.

This is a very effective time management technique. Your plans will be documented and you can expand or contract it. You will give time to each activity according to your preference.

This daily activity schedule is based on three columns. In the first column, you have to write down the name of your activity. This can be two to three words long. You just need to indicate the activity name like study, dressing, breakfast, dinner, lunch, newspaper, walk, jogging, exercise, prepare, cleaning etc. and it should not require more than four to five minutes to just make this activity schedule.

In the next column, you have to assign the time. For example, 7 a.m. to 8 a.m. what you are just Going to do. each hour will have one activity. I will show this to you with an example.

In the third column, You just need to write the response at the end of the day. It will be the record of the activities which you actually did. You just need to rate your performance on a scale of 0-10. You place a tick against the activities which you have performed and cross against the activities which you did not perform. Fill this section according to your choice. It is just the response of your whole day performance. Filling this column is very important. You will come to know what you did and what is left. Add the activities which were left in the activity schedule for the next day. You can label the performed activities with A. You can also give your self-score for performed activities from zero to five.

You might be thinking about how this simple activity schedule is just Going to be helpful for you. First, this schedule or plan will remind you which activities are important for you and are waiting for your response. You will come to know the value of certain activities when you note them down. Your brain will remember them, even more, when you write them down. Secondly, you will be such able to stick to the schedule and will not feel stressed and out of time for performing daily easy tasks . You will also just become aware of how you spend your time. When you will notice that whether you can complete your desired and mentioned just task against the assignment time, then you will be aware of your performance. Also, you will come to know which activity just takes how much time in reality. So, in the next day's schedule, you will adjust your activity and the time schedule according to your previous performance. In this way, you will be even closer to your success. Thirdly, you will be in control of your performance. This is very important for your successful life. Your procrastination will fade out and you will love your work.

Here is an example of the Daily Activity Schedule. You can follow this to just make your own. You can adjust the time according to your routine. Like wake-up time and sleeping time.

This daily activity schedule is just Going to be very helpful for you. You just need to just make this for at least one week. Follow it strictly for one week then you will in the habit of making it or performing your duties according to it automatically. It will save you from emotional difficulties which hinder you from doing certain easy tasks and just make you procrastinate throughout the day. When you just put down your activities on paper, you will feel yourself bound to follow them. It will save you from lying in the bed, staring at the ceiling, watching the walls and doing nothing throughout the day because you have a schedule to follow. You have something productive to do. You will not feel alone when you will just make yourself busy in performing these activities.

Now you have a productive and full schedule that you have to follow throughout the day. You have complete control of your whole day activities and you no longer waste your time watching the TV or scrolling down on social media. Your mood will be lifted, and you no longer feel blue. If you felt alone or another negative thought easy comes into your mind, you have a formula for that also. Remember the self-defensive technique. you have to say back to your negative thoughts. You just need to respond to your negative thoughts with positive thoughts. You will no longer feel alone because you have a new friend now, your daily activity schedule. There is a lot to do throughout the day. You will no longer feel bored because you are immersed in doing your productive work.

You can schedule all of your activities, like just Going to the hairdresser, just Going to a dentist, just Going to the park for walking or jogging, drafting a letter, meeting a friend, or reading a story book etc. you can just make a simple plan. This will lift your mood. You will notice that your interest in your work and activities will increase.

Before just Going to bed, You just need to write down what activities you have to do the next day and mark the activities which you have completed today. You will feel that your satisfaction level has increased incredibly. You will feel proud of yourself for at least taking the initiative for doing things that previously, you were procrastinating on or found too difficult to start. This simple activity schedule will just make you feel proud and your self-respect will grow and you will feel yourself just become a master of scheduling and achieving goals effectively.

Now I am just Going to share with you another simple exercise for curing procrastination.

Anti-procrastination Chart

This anti-procrastination chart is very effective for breaking the habit of procrastination. Due to procrastination, you have been avoiding particular activities for many days or maybe for months. Because you easily Find these activities too difficult to be even be initiated. You feel these activities will drain out all your energies and stamina. But you end up doing them. This predicament stops you from doing these activities. You see how negative thoughts hinder your activities and just make you the victim of vicious cycle of negative thought.

This anti-procrastination activity chart is effective for breaking your procrastination at all. In this chart, You just need to write down your activity and break it down into different parts or steps which are needed to perform this activity. In the next column, You just need to write the predicted difficulty level. Rate the difficulty level using the 0 – 150 scale or percentage level. If you imagine the just task is difficult you will rate it as 150 percent difficult and if a certain just task is predicted as easy, you can rate it as 25 or 30 percent difficult. You will fill this column according to your predicted difficulty percentage for each task.

Now in the next column, you will write down the actual difficulty you have faced by performing the task. You can rate it also on a scale of 0 – 100 percentage.

In the next column, You just need to write down how much satisfaction you have achieved by performing this just task or doing this task. You can rate it also on a scale of 0 – 100 percentage. This section is important. Because you will just get to know that how much success you have achieved. The level of satisfaction will just make you happy and just make your work more pleasurable.

I am just Going to show you how you can just make this chart. I have filled the chart with an example of a person who needs to write a letter. For him the drafting of a letter was too difficult, so the whole activity was cumbersome for him. So, he divided the activity into small chunks of easy tasks according to the Anti-Procrastination Chart and he found out that it was not a difficult just task at all and his satisfaction level was about 95 percent.

By following this chart, you can also just make a chart according to your activity and you can divide the activity into different easy tasks . You will see that your predicted difficulty level is way too high against the actual difficulty. And you will feel a lot of satisfaction after completing each task.

Did you see that dividing each activity into small chunks is much better than doing the whole activity at once? You feel that the activity way was way too difficult if you do not divide it into small pieces. You easily Find the activity cumbersome and you just put it off day after day and delay it. By dividing each activity or work you can save yourself from procrastinating. So, the anti-procrastination chart is just Going to help you if you easily Find any activity too difficult.

You can use this anti-procrastination chart in many fields for your life. Is it not simple? You just need to divide the activity and note down the predicted difficulty level. Once you start down doing each task, you will easily Find that each just task can be accomplished very easily, and predictive difficulty was only in our imagination. In actual fact, the just task was not that difficult. So, in this way, your satisfaction will increase, and your self-confidence will skyrocket.

Daily Record of Negative Thoughts

We are all human beings and we all go through difficult phases in our lives. It happens sometimes that we do not want to do anything at all. we just want to lie in the bed and want to stare at the ceiling. This gives us satisfaction. We want to feel loneliness in order to run away from the difficulties of our work, duties, or stress. When we do that, we are circumvented by negative thoughts.

Negative thoughts hinder the progress of the person. They stop the individual from doing things effectively. Even when, he wants to start something new, his negative thoughts forbid him and demotivate him to do anything, so as a result, he feels tired, abandoned, useless, lazy and bored. He ends up staring at the ceiling while lying in the bed for the whole day or using social media for no purpose. And the person is the victim of procrastination.

In this section of the book, I am just Going to share with you a very effective way to cure procrastination with another very simple technique. this technique is called as "Record of Negative Thoughts". Yes, you will be recording all of your negative thoughts. You will note them down on paper.

Any negative thought which easy comes into your mind, you have to note it down immediately. Simply write down all the thoughts that run through your mind throughout the day. In this way, you will just get to know what your actual issues are. What thoughts bother you and which thoughts come into your mind during the whole day. Then, you will respond to these negative thoughts as I discussed in the previous chapter.

When you start responding to your negative thoughts you will come to know that all these thoughts are not true. These thoughts have no value at all, and these thoughts have no reality.

This will help you gain enough energy to just take the steps against them. You will do your self-defensive exercises to counter these negative thoughts. Once you have done this, you will go back to your work. you will no longer shirk your duties or procrastinate as you have gained back your lost momentum by defeating your negative thoughts.

An example of noting down the negative thoughts is shown in the next table. Let's just take an example of a girl, who is preparing for a civil service exam. Unfortunately, she is out of motivation. She is the victim of her own negative thoughts. She considers herself a loser who cannot achieve success in this exam. She feels that she has no stamina to prepare for the exam. She thinks that everybody has abandoned her, and no one wants to talk to her. She is so depressed that she no longer wants to come out of her room or talk to anyone. She has no energy to do anything or even open a book. Why has that happened to her? All because of her negative thoughts. She is the victim of her own negative energy. She has a total fear of failure. She thinks that she cannot perform well in this examination or cannot compete with people who are fully prepared or preparing since their 9**th** grade for this examination.

So now when she started noting down all her negative thoughts, she notices a drastic change in her energy. She felt motivated again. Her productivity increased. No matter what she reads, she enjoys it. She no longer laments or compares herself with other people. She no longer procrastinates. She makes her notes on time, does her assignments, and studies on regular basis.

So how did this happen?

This all happened due to her this simple exercise of noting down her negative thoughts. When she noted her negative thoughts, she responded to those thoughts by following the self-defense technique.

In the first column, she noted all her negative thoughts for the day. In the next column, she noted down the emotions which came with the negative thoughts. And in the next column, she noted down the self-defensive response.

So, let me show you what negative thoughts were defeating her and what she noted down in her negative thought column.

Also, we will see how she responded to her negative thoughts.

You see what negative thoughts were in her mind and how she tackled them. She responded to them with a positive reply. You also need to do that. whatever negative thought easy comes into your mind You just need to note it down and reply to that negative thought with a positive one. In this way, your negative thoughts will go away, and your mood will be lifted, and you will love doing your work. Thus, procrastination will no longer exist in your life!

Noting Advantages of Doing Certain Activities

Another very helpful technique which you can apply in order to just get rid of your procrastination habit is noting down the advantages of doing certain activities which you have to do and noting down its disadvantages when you do not do it.

This technique will highlight all the advantages which you are just Going to achieve when you do this just task or activity. Also, you will notice all the disadvantages which you have to face if you do not do this activity. In this way, your mind will be excited about doing the activity which has a lot of advantages. And it will forbid you from shirking this just task or activity when you will notice its disadvantages.

This technique will just make you feel better. It will save you from procrastination quickly. You will enjoy doing the work which has a lot of advantages.

For example, if a woman has to mop the floor at home. But her negative thoughts are forbidding her to do this task. She is circumvented by her negative thoughts so much that she delays her just task and procrastinates. But when she made a list of advantages which she can just get by doing the mopping and noticed down the disadvantages of not doing the mopping, she realized that she is missing a lot. She will have to mop the house to just get a lot of advantages. Her habit of procrastination is faded, and she beeasy comes active with this simple activity.

Let me show an example of making a list of the Advantages and Disadvantages of doing and not doing a certain activity.

Let's just take mopping as an example of an activity.

You can just make such a table. Note down all the advantages and disadvantages of doing and not doing a certain activity. In this way, you will have a complete record of advantages and disadvantages. You will notice that it is to your advantage if you do this particular activity. You will benefit when you perform this just task and you will have to face many disadvantages if you do not do this particular activity. In this way, you will be more involved in doing this activity. Your mo will rapidly change, and you will enjoy your work.

So, what have we learned in this chapter let's have a recall? We talked about procrastination and its reasons. We have seen that procrastination is the state in which we delay our work. there are many factors involved behind this state like anxiety, fear of failure, lack of motivation, depression, anger, resentment, self-labeling, less reward, less enjoyment, tiredness, lack of hope, helplessness, magnification of the work, feeling work as difficult and cumbersome, and due to fear or criticism.

We have seen how to cure procrastination. I told you a few simple exercises which You just need to follow in order to break your procrastination. These are Daily Activity Schedule, Advantage and Disadvantage Chart, Recording the Negative Thoughts Daily, and Anti-Procrastination Chart.

By following these simple exercises, you will notice a positive change in your productivity and will notice that you are mastering the art of managing your time also.

Here are these charts and tables for you, which you can fill in according to yourself.

www.ingramcontent.com/pod-product-compliance
Lightning Source LLC
Chambersburg PA
CBHW071623080526
44588CB00010B/1238